Ameer-Hasaan Walton

My Historically

BLACK PURPOSE

Foreword By Dr. Theresa Price,
Maurice Robinson M.A. & Dr. Raymond Shorter

MY HISTORICALLY BLACK PURPOSE

AMEER-HASAAN WALTON

Table of Contents

FOREWORD

MAURICE ROBINSON M.A.

Historically Black Colleges and Universities provide an opportunity to witness young people from around the world collaborate, produce new information and contribute to the global community. At the same time, these students are being developed culturally and intellectually in ways that embrace their history and heritage.

All over the world, we see people of color suffering from poverty, lack of education and lack of skill. I had become numb to all the rhetoric painting the people who look like me as inept, dangerous, or incapable. I never thought I would see the beauty that met my eyes the day I walked on the campus of Bowie State University, the same as one would see strolling through Florida International or Maryland Eastern Shore I imagine.

Thousands of young people from the African diaspora learning and contributing to all the fields that make up our society today. In undergrad, I had friends who were studying history and government. Others studied nursing, biology, mathematics, business, accounting, and everything else you could imagine. The beauty of this visual is the potential scene it sets for a world where black people possess all the skills and institutional knowledge they need to problem solve different issues that have plagued their communities.

Where else in the world can this be found as a daily activity? Every day gives you the resounding feeling that you're building something, something that will grow and live on after your time at the university and in life.

This is important!

More crucial than the things you do in life are the people you do them with. I have two degrees, and I am finishing my third as I write this foreword. I have one from an HBCU and my two graduate-level degrees from Predominantly White Institutions (PWI's). Given this, I do not hesitate to claim the preeminence of my time and experiences at my historically black college. Here my paradigm and approach to life took root, it has allowed me to explore mentally and scholarly in a way that made the transition of me branching out into the paradigms of other institutions more natural.

These black colleges and universities are not only to be revered for their historical contributions. In the present day, students at these universities are doing amazing things. Our students are making vast contributions to medicine, domestic and international business, politics, agriculture, and technology industries. The institutions are growing in population and size; The resumes of schools like Howard and Hampton University stack up against the most prestigious ivy league institutions.

If you are looking for a reason to attend an HBCU, I encourage you to ask the 300,000 students currently enrolled at historically black colleges and universities today, or the millions of alumni throughout the world who perpetually celebrate their universities.

FOREWORD

DR. RAYMOND SHORTER

Imagine a place where you will go and experience an abundant amount of love, peace, unity, and joy. A place where you will acquire knowledge, wisdom, visions, and goals. A place where you will explore communication skills, networking skills, leadership skills, and social skills. A place where you will express who you are and become whom you want to be. A place where you will engage in opportunities that will empower you to manifest the essence of your existence. A place where you will experience rites of passage for manhood and womanhood. A place where you will build upon your eternal legacy. A place where you will experience the true meaning of heaven on earth. These experiences are deeply embedded throughout every Historically Black College and University.

Therefore, Historically Black Colleges and Universities are places where you know you will experience love and support from people who want to help you succeed. You know that you will develop brotherhood and sisterhood relationships with hundreds or even thousands of people who look like you. You will build upon these extended family members by adding new members consisting of powerful and long-lasting relationships with other students, faculty, staff, administrators and community leaders. You know that you will develop skills that prepare you to change the world and rule the world. Thus, as you embrace upon your journey at a Historically Black College and University, you know that you will have a magnificent experience that will forever change your life.

With that said, you must understand that Historically Black Colleges and Universities will guide you toward gaining knowledge of yourself so you will master that knowledge of yourself. You will become a top-notch scholar cultivating your writing skills, research skills, critical thinking skills, and public speaking skills. You will become one of the most influential leaders in the world by engaging in leadership opportunities while executing your visions and goals. You will learn about the greatness of who you are, which is a beautiful and brilliant spiritual scholar; who will continue to enhance your spirituality to a higher level of spiritual consciousness so you can build a better world.

Finally, as I pay homage to the great experiences that you will have at Historically Black Colleges and Universities, I would like to express that I am so proud, honored, and privileged to have been a graduate of the Masters of Business Administration program at the illustrious Hampton University. Hampton University provided me with every opportunity to become successful and embrace my love for Black people throughout the world. More importantly, my journey at Hampton University allowed me to truly experience black excellence, which is literally heaven on earth.

FOREWORD

DR. THERESA PRICE

As the Founder of Black College Expo™, I have had the opportunity to meet some of the brightest, most innovative, creative, intellectual, capable human beings all connected with the same thread...products of an HBCU. However, I did not attend an HBCU, because I didn't know about HBCUs. Thus, Black College Expo™ was created so all students of all colors would see the history and legacy of black colleges. I can say that I can clearly see the difference between HBCU grads and PWI grads.

In most cases, there's definitely more "meat and potatoes" with HBCU grads. They have more stamina, they seem very grounded, and very confident in who they are and what they are about. HBCUs seem to give our students more power to feel empowered. It's not a race thing...it's a valued thing. Pretty much every HBCU alumni I have come across, seem to know their value and know that they are appreciated, and it doesn't matter who they go up against, they are confident that they too, can bring it!

I have seen students get a chance to go to an HBCU with a GPA as low as a 1.5, however, by the time they graduate their grades were higher, their self-confidence was higher, understanding their self-value was acknowledged, their work ethic was excellent and they knew "they mattered." HBCUs offer a safe-haven for students to learn who they are as young men and women. These institutions help students find themselves and their purpose on earth, offer a great education, both street and book knowledge, helps students to learn and grow into their best selves, while at the same time teach them how to navigate and find their way, or as my ancestors would say "fin for themselves". HBCUs are needed more now than ever to connect students to their past, present, and future. Author Ameer Walton has been serving as our Black College Expo™ "Power of Me" Tour Manager around the country, which visits as many as 12 cities around the United States annually. This book represents the experience he has been sharing with students around the world. Ameer has TRANSFORMED from not knowing who or why; to knowing exactly who he is and knowing his PURPOSE.

INTRODUCTION

The HBCU experience can best be described as a pot of gumbo. If you don't know, gumbo is a delicious New Orleans dish that has absolutely everything you find in a black kitchen in one pot, mixed up and seasoned well with Zatarans! Within this pot, you'll find shrimp, crab, sausage, and plenty other tasty necessities to make your gumbo great. Just like Gumbo, every HBCU is different. However, they all feed the spirit of the black community. My pot was seasoned with great culture, hearty meat of knowledge, healthy veggies in the form of teachers/administration and last but certainly not least, the foundation of rice which is our alumni and ancestors. If you're getting hungry, GOOD! This food for thought is the best meal you'll ever get.

The way I ended up at my HBCU was not the easy way. Before I go any further, I want to make a few points abundantly clear. To anyone in the process of choosing a University, pick the school that fits YOU! Not your Parents! Not your friends! Not your significant other. Just you! Listen to the people who have your best interest at the forefront. Those won't always be the people they should be or the people you expect them to be. It's up to you to use your intuition to see which people to listen to and make the best decision for yourself. I had a unique situation; I was a basketball player who was one of the top 30 players in northern California at one point.

I ate, slept and breathed basketball. My dad and I worked out all the time; sports was my world. Unfortunately, when I got to my senior year, my grades looked worse than President Trump's approval rating. I ended up graduating with barely a 2.0-grade point average. The scholarship opportunities I had, no longer existed. I thought my only choice was to go to a junior college, then take up one of the scholarship opportunities. My mother didn't believe or agree with my choice. She sent me on the 100% College Prep HBCU Tour. I didn't want to go on the tour at first, but as usual, my mom knew best.

That trip was the best thing that could have ever happened to me. I got to see and experience HBCU culture firsthand. They called them Universities, but to me, these were black utopias. I was surrounded by black excellence:

black teachers, students, faculty, staff, administration, and chefs. Everybody was black. What stuck out to me was the confidence and prestige everyone displayed. I wanted to be a part of this. I arrived at the University that would eventually take my heart towards the end of the trip, Bowie State University. It was a beautiful campus, and the students and faculty we met with were some of the most friendly. It felt like home. I couldn't believe I was thinking about attending a school that I just discovered. The coach even said he had a spot for me on the basketball team. Everything was lining up perfectly. I'd be lying if I didn't tell you the ratio was 28 girls to every guy, that absolutely had an impact on my decision. I made my choice to attend Bowie State University less than a month before I graduated. If you had told me when I first got to High School, that a University I would find out about a month before I graduated was going to change my life, I would have looked at you crazy.

I decided not to play basketball during my first year because I wanted to focus on my grades. I ended that year with a 3.5 GPA. I was about to make another life-changing decision; I didn't want to play basketball anymore. If you had seen the looks on some of the people's faces in my neighborhood when I told them I quit playing, you would have thought I had committed the most sinister crime. I could tell these people didn't know the whole me, or who I had the potential to become. I was more motivated than ever to show them, but most importantly, I wanted to show myself. I'm the author of the story of my life. Nobody else had the right to write my pages. The days of getting pressured into how I was going to live my life was over. I hope ALL of you are writing each chapter to your life story, if not, start today.

The rest of my time at Bowie State University, I dedicated myself to becoming the best mental, physical and spiritual form of myself. I had experiences and opportunities I would have never received at a predominantly white institution (I know because I attended UCLA for a year). I became a resident assistant and co-founded my organization, Black Male Agenda. I also became Mr. Bowie State University, I got an award for Man of the Year, I was one of 3 selected to the Black Executive Exchange Program, I've met with Barack Obama, Nikki Giovani, I was a special guest of Minister Farrakhan 3 times including at the 20th Anniversary of the Million Man March. And I graduated with a GPA over 3.0. This wasn't by accident, the mentors I met my first semester began molding me into the man they knew I could be; they never rested or took it easy on me until they saw results. This was a custom-made growing up process that couldn't be duplicated anywhere else. HBCUs have a way of bringing out the purpose you didn't know existed and manifesting it into a reality.

This book is to help you understand how HBCUs will bring out your purpose and what you'll need to do to make reality out of that purpose. We all have God-given gifts that are worth billions monetarily and spiritually. You must use those gifts to change the world. Changing the world isn't an easy task, but it is attainable; you must be bold, brilliant, fearless and move with purpose. The secret to success is constancy of purpose. I've narrowed the HBCU Transformation down to 10 points that will hopefully help you decide which pot of gumbo you want to choose. Before we get started, I leave you with a quote.

"And I hope that five years and 10 years from now, I'll be a better man, a more mature man, a wiser man, a more humble man and a more spirited man to serve the good of my people and the good of humanity."

The Honorable Minister, Louis Farrakhan

PART I

LISTEN TO THE ELDERS

"The wisdom of our elders like gold can be found deep within their mountains of knowledge or flowing amongst the streams of their actions."

- Alex Payton

What's the difference between being smart and being wise? If you're blessed enough to have your grandparents around, it's a great question to ask them. Being smart is knowing information, being knowledgeable and up-to-date with the times. Wisdom knows how the world works, knowing how to apply knowledge within the matrix to crack the code. They say a smart person never makes the same mistake, but a wise person doesn't need to make a mistake, they learn from those who did. Your parents, grandparents, aunties, uncles, brothers, sisters have all had life experiences that you haven't. They've experienced the good, bad and ugly in life that you haven't been on the earth long enough to understand. But, if you're wise enough, you'll not only listen but apply. My mom told me her only regret when it came to school was attending San Francisco State University instead of Howard University. She forced me to go on an HBCU college tour so I wouldn't make the same mistake she made. That college tour convinced me to go to Bowie State University, which changed my life forever.

I wouldn't be the man I am today without my HBCU. So, my mother's wisdom plus my work ethic and vision led to the most significant college experience I could have imagined. As young people, we have a habit of thinking once we've reached a certain age that we're an adult. When I was 18, you couldn't tell me anything. I thought I had it all figured out. However, manhood and womanhood aren't defined by your age, it's determined by your ability to prioritize and handle your obligations responsibly and to the best of your ability. The elders at my University quickly helped me understand what I thought I knew was equivalent to a crumb in a bakery. When I arrived at Bowie State University as a freshman, I was coming in as someone who had underperformed in the classroom. My dad told me I was coming back home if I messed up again. I didn't take that seriously enough. When you get to your HBCU, you'll learn about homecoming! It's a life-changing party from sun up to sun down for a whole week. Free food, free parties, comedy shows, and step shows. It was the best thing I had ever experienced. I'm from California. We don't have any HBCUs, so for me, it was baptism by fire.

I decided not to go to class much that week and midterm grades came out the week after homecoming. Of course, at this crazy week-long celebration, I didn't think I'd run into any of my teachers. Wrong. I was at yard fest (A Big free concert thousands of people show up for), having a good time. I feel a tap on my shoulder. It's Mr. Shorter, my freshman seminar teacher. Before I can get a word out, he says, "You haven't been in my class this week." Then he walks off. I didn't think I was going to see anyone else. I feel another tap on my shoulder. I couldn't believe it, Dr. Miller, my African American History teacher says, "Haven't seen you in a while" and left me right where I stood. I knew this wasn't going to end well, but I didn't estimate how bad. The following week, I saw 2 F's on my midterm for Freshman Seminar and African American History. I was shocked and scared because I didn't want to go home. I was having visions of my dad telling me to pack my bags. I couldn't let this become a reality. I had to take action; I went to talk to my two teachers to get this situation resolved. I told both of them I thought I deserved at least a

C because I turned in all my work. You would have thought they talked to each other because they gave me the same explanation for my F's. They both said, "You're only getting one of two grades in my class, an A or an F. I don't allow mediocrity in my classroom. Anything between an A and an F is mediocre. So, you're either going to do exactly what I tell you to do and get an A, or you're going to do what you want to do and get an F."

Those conversations from Dr. Miller and Dr. Shorter changed my life. I had lost out on scholarship opportunities for sports because of my grades, even then I thought I could get through college doing the same thing. But, nobody wants an average car, girlfriend, boyfriend or food. So why would I want to walk around with mediocre grades? That wasn't me, and I knew it wasn't me, so I decided then to listen to what my elders said and be extraordinary in all that I do. I dedicated myself to making sure that everything my name was attached to would be luxurious. I ended up getting an "A" in both of those classes. To this day, I thank those two men for seeing how smart I was and using their wisdom to bring out the excellence in me. You have to understand that your smarts plus the wisdom of your elders is an unstoppable force. It's a two-sided equation that you must humble yourself to realize. My elders helped elevate me from average to excellent, and they can do the same for you.

PART II

CARRY ON TRADITION (LEGACY)

"We all have a past, we all have a future. Our job is to understand who we are in that time and contribute to the divine legacy. Legacy equals tradition which equals growth which equals life."

- Marcus White

Every race has pillars supporting their legacy. Those pillars serve as the foundation for future generations. We're supposed to carry on a tradition so generations who come after us can have a full understanding of the greatness they inherit. Pride breeds confidence and confidence breeds success. Knowing you come from a legacy of importance, and having an obligation to carry on that legacy, builds the psyche to a level of belief in self that is imperative to reaching greatness. I'm a firm believer to know where you're going; you have to see where you've been. Unfortunately, black people in the United States have been stripped of traditions because of slavery and systemic oppression. Most of our families don't have traditions passed down from ancient times. Our textbooks from the time we enter the school system are filled with white faces. For black people, that breeds detachment to education and indifference to culture. White people display a high level of passion for American History because of the way they're represented. They get to open up history books and see themselves as inventors, politicians and business owners. They look at their people living the American dream. Watch the joy Irish people have on St. Patrick's Day or Mexican people have on Cinco de Mayo. It's because they have a sense of tradition.

What black holiday do black people universally get behind and celebrate? Don't say Kwanzaa. We have endured unthinkable trauma and are in dire need of history reprogramming and representation. We have way more history than slavery, marching for freedom and Barak Obama. We have built pyramids, mastered science, mathematics and have countless inventions. But, until the story of the hunt is told by the lion, the tale of the hunt will always glorify the hunter. It's our job to make sure our complete stories are told. If you don't believe representation has an impact, think about how the black community reacted when "Black

Panther" came out; and that was fiction. For the majority of us, our education on black history starts in a slave ship, goes to a romanticized version of slavery, fast forwards to the Emancipation Proclamation (Did not free slaves), fast forwards to Martin Luther King and then finally, fast forwards to Barak Obama. First off, those are some significant gaps, second off, if you start Black history from slavery, you're cutting off the head of a glorious body of black traditions and culture. The body can't move without the head. I hope all of you have seen the movie Hidden Figures. It tells the story of 3 black women who calculated the trajectory of Apollo 11 in 1961. It's a great story about 3 American heroines. Their story didn't appear in any of my history books.

Every HBCU has hidden figures that will blow your mind. The contributions we've put forward in world history can't fit into a library.

Most of us don't know when our elementary, middle school or high schools founding dates are because we don't care. The first thing that happens when you get to your HBCU is a thorough breakdown of the history of your school. My University was started in a Baptist church by a few black women in 1865, a time where they could have been killed for trying to educate black people. They dared to do it anyway, and today, that University holds over 5,000 students. I take pride every day in knowing the sacrifice those women made paved the way for me to learn comfortably. Their legacy lives through me and the rest of the students who walk the campus. If you take on the responsibility of carrying on the tradition that is instilled at your HBCU, I can guarantee it will be a beautiful journey unlike any other. You get to fill the shoes of great black leaders that have laid the foundation of the world. The best part of filling the shoes of legends is getting the opportunity to raise the bar that they have set. It's a challenge that I wouldn't trade for anything. I know I stand on the shoulders of greatness, and I know that my shoulders will also be used as the foundation for future generations to carry on the tradition.

PART III

OPPORTUNITIES

"Be a maverick and dare to be your best self. The greatest leaders are the ones who said yes to the opportunities others said no to. Don't ever be afraid to enhance your skill set and network."

- Darrius Gwynn

Everyone needs a chance. Some people wait their whole lives trying to find a space where they have the opportunity to showcase themselves, be themselves, hear themselves and become themselves. As a High School senior, I was on that historically black college tour looking for an opportunity. In my heart, I knew I didn't deserve a chance based on my grades. However, I knew I was more than just those grades on the paper. I was involved in my community, extracurricular activities and I had a great personality. I didn't need every school to believe in me; I needed one. One of the highlights of going on the black college tour was the opportunity to sit down with the admission counselors and explain my story to them. No, I didn't do the best in high school, but if I got the opportunity, I would make sure I was remembered as one of the great ones to step foot on that campus. They gave me the opportunity I needed, and it changed my life. But, I know I turned that campus around as well. So, what started as an opportunity became a partnership.

The admissions representatives that approved me believed in me as a person, and they wanted me to bring that same energy to the campus. They knew I was a leader and every University needs leaders. I was a business major, and one principle we use is Return On Investment (R.O.I.). When someone invests, you always want to make a profit. If you put in a dollar, you want to get at least two dollars back. In this case, they wanted an asset to their university. If you're reading this, I know you have skills that can make you an asset to any University and the world. I also believe in being in an environment that gives you the chance to be yourself unapologetically. During my first semester in college, I heard about nooses being hung up at the University Of Maryland. I also had friends who went to other predominantly white institutions that dealt with harassment from campus police, teachers and students because they were black. There's nothing like being embraced and nurtured for your blackness. At your HBCU, you don't have to worry about other students calling police on you for walking on campus or playing your music loud. You can exist in complete peace for four years.

I often talk to parents about their kids attending HBCUs. Their diversity concerns always arise during these conversations. I ask them, "Have your kids had an opportunity to explore all the diversity amongst black people?" There are plenty of people who have never met a black Muslim, a black Jew, black people from Africa, Europe, the Caribbean, South America, never spoke to a gay black person or met a black president of a University. How important is to be amongst other races when you haven't had the opportunity to explore your own? The most confident people walking this planet are the ones who are knowledgeable of themselves. You gain that knowledge by giving yourself the opportunity to grow holistically. I've had the privilege of traveling with the Black College Expo. This life-changing event brings together hundreds of HBCUs who are looking to give students the opportunity to prove themselves. Why not attend a place that wants to provide you with an opportunity, that wants you to be yourself and express yourself? Maybe it's time we stop trying to fit in and instead, go with the institutions that were tailor-made for us. I think it's time we go to the schools that give us the best opportunity to live our best life. Don't waste that opportunity; you never know if it will come back around.

PART IV

PREPARATION

"Let your lessons and experiences fertilize your evolution and growth. Wisdom stems from honoring and embracing the process in order to bloom."

- Desiree Sealey

In the words of GLC, "Proper Preparation Prevents Poor Performance." Don't spend your whole life praying for a blessing you aren't prepared to receive. Don't disappoint yourself and others who believe in you by not preparing as if your life depended on it. The great thing about your HBCU is that it is such an encouraging atmosphere that you will get pulled in plenty of different directions. Come to this party! Join this club! Join this fraternity! Join this sorority! Can you speak at this event?! The more well-known you get and the more your abilities are on display, the more involved you will become.

The responsibility that comes with that is making sure you prepare for what's most important to you. As a student, your first obligation is getting the best grades possible. That means studying longer to ensure you get that "A"! It also means not starting on a semester project the night before its due. I've been guilty of this. Preparation comes down to ensuring the least amount of stress as possible in your life. The more prepared you are, the fewer surprises there will be that stress you out. Some things in life are uncontrollable and will require you to do your best work in a short amount of time. However, you don't want this to become the norm. I was heavily involved on campus, but I was successful because of my preparation. At an HBCU, people let you know how you performed; whether it's good or bad. You don't want to be on the wrong end of that, but there is no greater feeling than being on the right end of it. We talk a lot about the family atmosphere, and I'll talk about it later in the book. Part of what makes a family atmosphere so beneficial is the accountability that is placed upon you to deliver a great product. As a family, we have to be able to keep it real with each other.

My HBCU showed me how to prepare on a professional level. Showing up on time for a presentation isn't enough. You show up with ample time to run through all your notes, make sure the equipment works and analyze the room set up. I was taught a supreme level of preparation. That extra preparation I learned to implement in every facet of my life was a significant piece of all the accomplishments I got while in college and especially after I got out. Poor performances can follow you for a lifetime. Don't miss out on future opportunities because of a lack of preparation. Getting an interview for a job is great, actually getting the job is even better. Getting the job is excellent, elevating higher and higher in that company is the best. Every day of your life brings a new task that requires greater preparation. It never stops, the stakes get higher, and the blessings get bigger, so prepare better. You only get one chance to make a first impression. Take it seriously.

PART V

HURDLES

"The most important purpose of an obstacle in life is to show you how much faith you need to get past it. No obstacle can stop what you believe in your heart."

- Alex "Ptah" Lambert III

If you don't learn to embrace the journey and all the trials and tribulations that come with it, you'll never reach the goals you're trying to attain. Beyonce and the rest of Destiny's Child lost a singing competition when they were teenagers, Michael Jordan didn't make the basketball team his Freshman year. They never quit. I've failed lessons and not been able to afford classes, but I stuck with it and finished up. When you want something, it doesn't matter what gets in your way or how long it takes to accomplish it. You understand the value in that struggle, and you accept it. In return, not only will you achieve your goals, but you'll also become a better person! It's easy to do when you live by this Notorious B.I.G. quote, "Stay far from timid/Only make moves if your heart's in it/And live the phrase Sky's the limit." The most important part of that statement is, "Only make moves if your heart's in it." When you're passionate about something, you don't need the motivation to get it done; you just do it. When I was at the end of my freshman year of college heading into my sophomore year, my family was struggling financially, and we didn't know how I was going to pay for school. All I knew was I was going to try to get my tuition as low as possible to help my parents. This was a big hurdle, but hurdles also help you with another H word. Hustle!

I was asking everyone I could what ways I could get my tuition lowered. I ended up getting recommended to become a resident assistant. A resident assistant lives in the dorms and chaperones the underclassman. I ended up applying and got chosen. The job took care of my room and board and all my books for the year. That ended up cutting my tuition in half. We ended up getting the rest of the money I needed thanks to my mom and my auntie Poopie. A few years later, I didn't have the money to go to school, and there was nothing we could do about it. I was out of school for a year. I felt horrible, didn't know why I was the one who couldn't go to school. I had to watch all my friends having fun and graduating. I was happy for them, but I was hurt I couldn't be there. Instead of complaining, I registered for a class at UCLA to keep my mind moving, and I ended up having a great experience. What I learned at that time was how much I missed my University and how great my HBCU was. As illustrious as UCLA was, it wasn't home. Bowie was where my heart was, and I worked extremely hard to do everything I could to get back to school. I ended up graduating a year and a half later. It took me seven years to get my degree, hurdles all the way through. I had plenty of reasons to quit along my journey, but I never gave in. Sure, I wanted to hear my name called on that stage because it was a symbol of the hard work. But, the journey meant so much more. My family hustling to get me money, me hustling to get money, my friends supporting me, the all-night study sessions, the doubters, the believers. It all helped me become a better man. The journey was so valuable I forgot how difficult it was by the time I made it through. I was just thankful for the process because I knew those sacrifices would help me reach a life full of happiness.

PART VI

RITES OF PASSAGE

"Nothing in life worth having is easily obtained, and the joy of achievement through merit is sweet. This is the virtue of rites of passage"

- Brian Whitehead

Throughout history, different people from all across the world have participated in rites of passage. These ceremonies have been used as a milestone for the youth to step into positions of power. Power is not necessarily monetary or military. It's the power of intellect and understanding. When you reach this, you know you can maneuver in a room with anyone, hold a conversation with anyone and demand respect from anyone. The journey after the transformation last a lifetime, but the road for your life is defined during this process. When do black men and black women come of age? When do we step into manhood and womanhood? What is the process? Does age dictate it? Do we become men and women when we reach 13, 16, 18, 21, maybe 25? Have you ever wondered what the criteria are to be considered a man or woman correctly? I always thought it was interesting how my Latino friends had a Quinceañera or how my Jewish friends had a Bar Mitzvah or Bat Mitzvah. To my knowledge, black people didn't have anything equivalent to those ceremonies. Some people say a Beautillion or Cotillion is a rite of passage for black people. However, you usually need to be associated with Jack and Jill or the Links to participate. So naturally, most black people never get the chance to be included. I was fortunate enough to be a part of a Beautillion, and it was a great experience! But my true Rites of Passage came while attending my HBCU.

If you haven't already, see the movie 300. The opening scene starts with a young boy getting trained by his mother and father and eventually being sent out into the wilderness to fight the elements and animals. Once he's completed all these tasks, he comes back a king. This is what the HBCU experience is like for young black men and women. Not as extreme, of course. To be able to leave home and surround yourself with strangers is an experience that can't be simulated. It's a mystery novel that ends up becoming the most excellent story ever told. Learning a new area is great because these HBCUs are in such historic cities that the history of accomplishments by black folks is endless. You end up embracing the city and all that comes with it. The life lessons that you learn from friends that become family are priceless; managing relationships with teachers you aren't fond of, falling in love and finding yourself. Having your thoughts and ideas challenged. Figuring out what you're going to eat with nothing in your pocket. Balancing all these tasks and keeping a social life is one of the best survival guides you'll ever have. The Rites Of passage isn't all about fighting what's around you. It's about breaking down what's inside of you; the battle of thyself is the toughest battle but to know thyself is the greatest reward. In Naim Akbar's book, Vision for Black Men, he talks about the transformation into manhood being similar to a caterpillar becoming a butterfly.

I think this is the best way to describe the HBCU process from start to finish. Everyone wants to reach butterfly status but to spread your wings, you must go through the cocoon. The cocoon symbolizes your Rites Of Passage. It's not cute or pretty, but it's a necessary step in the evolution of your true self. The cocoon shields the caterpillar from the world so the growth can take place; similar to the way your university will protect you. While you're inside your cocoon, the transformation takes place.

When the caterpillar is ready to show the world its entire beauty, it must break free from the cocoon, unassisted. Once it does, the transformation is complete, and you can spend the rest of your days spreading your wings. Embrace the four years the HBCU cocoon can provide, then display your beauty.

PART VII

LEADERSHIP

"Service with purpose. Serve by growing the talent around you to potential. Be the catalyst for concerted action to realize."

- Julian Walker-Rodwell

Leadership isn't for the weak. It's scary. It's fun. It's exhausting. It's time-consuming. It's selfless. It's strategic. It's fulfilling. It takes a confident person who isn't afraid to be true to what they believe in regardless of what the majority thinks. They hold themselves accountable for their actions, as well as their team. They don't need the glory of their name being on the front page. Martin Luther King Jr. had a sermon called, "Drum Major Instinct." In this sermon, he described people who desire to be in the limelight but lack the passion for putting in the work necessary to be a leader. For the true leader, the glory is in knowing the goals are complete. It has to begin with an honest conversation with yourself.

Why do I want to be a leader? Am I fit to be a

leader? Who am I attempting to lead? Will they follow me? The why is the most critical question; this question is the seed from which your fruit will blossom. If the seed is rotten, the fruit will be rotten. Your motive must be pure, don't do it because it sounds nice or would look good on your resume. Do it because there is a cause that means something to you. You shouldn't need anyone to define it for you because it will come straight from your heart. It takes an in-depth look in the mirror to say if you are fit to lead. We all have some friends, family or acquaintances who are not fit to lead because of their lifestyle choices. You can't be one person half the day and another person the other half. Leadership isn't a day job you take Monday - Friday from 9 am to 5 pm, then you get to the weekend, and become a different person. Leadership is more than a position; it's a lifestyle. So everyone can't lead from the front; sometimes you have to assist. That assisting is essential to overall success and is also a form of leadership because it shows responsibility and commitment to get the job done. Leaders are all over the place. There are more behind the scenes than in the light. Choose the form of leadership that best fits your life, not your personal gain.

The "who"? Do you know the who and does the who know you? While I was at my HBCU, I wanted to be a leader to everyone, but there was a special place in my heart for the young black men on campus. We were having a tough time with retention of the black males after their first year. I wanted to tackle this problem head-on, but the last thing I wanted to be was someone who only showed up when they were wrong or weren't doing well. I was committed, so I had to make myself available. That's why I requested to work with Freshman males when I was a resident assistant. They wouldn't have a choice but to know me and vice versa if we lived together for a whole year. We had a great year building our relationship, it was a beautiful experience because I saw myself in all of them and I knew what it would take to help them be as successful as possible. If nothing else, I wanted to plant seeds in each of them that would help them understand they had a purpose whether they stayed at school or not. The "Who" has two parts because outside of knowing them, you have to understand them. It's irresponsible to try and lead a group of people who you haven't invested the time into fully understanding. These people are trusting you with the path of their lives; you can't take that lightly, do your research. That also means not bringing your insecurities and shortcomings into their lives, never punish those you are trying to lead because you haven't dealt with your pain.

Will they follow? There aren't many people who can predict if the people they are attempting to lead will support them. There isn't a recipe available to get everyone the exact results they want. Most times, it's an undying passion that you have to meet head-on regardless of the outcome. There are elections, pageants and different kinds of contest every year and more people lose than win. These are some of the questions you have to ask yourself. Are those titles what makes you a leader? Do those titles make you a good leader? Are there more leaders without titles? If you fail to win a position and quit your path of leadership, you may not be ready for what leadership truly entails. You have to be willing to do whatever it takes to accomplish the goals. Fall seven times and get up 8. While I was a resident assistant, I wanted to step into a more significant capacity of leadership, so I decided to run for Mr. Black & Gold. Mr. Black & Gold served under Mr. Bowie State on the royal court. Every position on the royal court is very prestigious in the HBCU community, and they come with a lot of power on campus. Mr. Black and Gold is supposed to be for someone who represented the males on campus and would be a role model for what black men were supposed to represent. I ran for the position, and I lost. I thought I was cheated because I knew no one represented the males in a positive perspective the way I did. I was very disappointed, and I felt like I had failed. But, I had to think about it holistically. I was directly changing the lives of young black males on campus in ways people had never seen before through my work as a resident assistant and as president of my organization, Black Male Agenda. I didn't need that position, that position needed me. I was already a leader, and I knew that. That position just wasn't meant for me. Another brother had earned the spot, so I had to respect it, and he did a great job. But I'm not a quitter; I wanted to prove I could get that position and shake things up. I ended up running for Mr. Bowie (the position above Mr. Black & Gold) the following year, and I won. What God has for you, no one can take away.

Some people are in more popular positions of leadership than others, but they are all equally important, we are all equally important with the ability to influence and lead. We talk about how successful Jay-Z is, but do you know who Dame Dash, Kareem Biggs, and Jaz-O are? We talk about how successful Martin Luther King Jr. was, but do you know who Hosea Williams, Ralph Abernathy, Andrew Young, Henry Groskinsky, William Campbell and Ben Branch were? Define your leadership and stick to it. My HBCU instilled the selfless side of leadership in me. Your Legacy will follow you forever, as it should, but outside of personal goals, the real intent of a leader should be to create more leaders. These positions have limited time, our time on this earth is limited. The way you leave a legacy of leadership is building a culture of leadership. Demand leadership from everyone around you especially the young people who look up to you because when leadership becomes contagious, success becomes consistent. Make sure when you leave whatever leadership position you are in, you've not only set the bar higher than ever before, you've also laid the foundation for those coming behind you to rise and raise the bar even higher than you did.

PART VIII

EXCELLENCE

"To excel is to habitually practice the acts of reinventing and re-motivating yourself to be better each day. We are all created individually, and there's no universal standard for achievement; we define it for ourselves. Allow yourself to walk in your purpose and define your life on your terms."

- Ayana Harlee

The process of digging for diamonds is long and tedious. You have to go deep into the dirt to find the diamonds. That's the same process it takes for finding excellence in yourself. My HBCU helped me perfect the excellence mind state. Proverbs, chapter 23, verse 7: "As a man thinketh in his heart, so is he." James Allen does a great job expounding on this in his book, "As a man thinketh." If you believe it, then you can achieve it. Set goals for yourself. Everything won't happen on schedule, but it will be right on time. You must strive for something incredible. It won't be easy, but if it were, you wouldn't appreciate the accomplishment. Like Fredrick Douglas said, "without a struggle, there can be no progress."You have to look at excellence as a lifelong journey, always challenge yourself. Whenever you feel like you've made it to the mountaintop and there's nothing else to do, stagnation comes. Being idle is the death of your maturation, so push yourself and enjoy the ride. I told you the story of my grades with my teachers not allowing mediocrity. What I loved at my HBCU was the excellence that was displayed every day. It was so motivating seeing so many young black future entrepreneurs, doctors, lawyers, psychologists and teachers working to achieve excellence in their craft. All the black excellence not only motivates you to accomplish your goals, but it makes you even happier to be a black man or woman knowing that people like you are going to be shaping the world. One of the best feelings is knowing that those same people you are hustling with in college are going to hold you accountable to reach excellence. The adjustment you have to make is going from wanting excellence to expecting excellence. You have to claim your victories immediately. Muhammad Ali said, "I am the greatest, I said that even before I knew I was." That has to be your thought process. Expect excellence from yourself, then hold those around you to that same excellence.

If you allow people around you to produce

mediocre work, the energy that should be used to achieve excellence will be wasted trying to motivate people who don't have the same drive you have. Rid yourself of individuals who don't demand excellence from themselves; they'll be immovable anchors on your journey to excellence. As I said in the previous chapter, I lost my run at Mr. Black & Gold. I had to go back to the drawing board. I viewed that loss as me not aiming high enough. So, I decided to campaign for Mr. Bowie State University. For those who aren't familiar with the Royal Court system. All HBCUs have a Queen of the university, and most of them have a King and Queen; the position is titled Mr. or Miss whatever the name of the university is. These positions were created to show the beauty black people had to offer because we weren't allowed to participate in the Miss America pageants at one point. If you hold one of these positions, you are treated like royalty. You are the face of the campus. You get a new wardrobe, you get special seating at the sports games, for the Homecoming football game, you get brought on the field with a million dancers and a band playing around you. It feels like "Coming to America" in real life. But, with great power comes great responsibility. When you ask for excellence, people expect excellence from you as well. You become a voice for people who can't speak, and you're a 24/7 leader. To me, that embodied excellence. You must be a unique person to enjoy life, be a voice for the people and handle daily responsibilities. It was a challenge I wanted because it demanded excellence. I could leave my mark on campus and also be a part of an extraordinary legacy. What I realized during my campaign was that I had been moving in excellence my entire time at Bowie State.

The people I left great impressions on, my involvement on campus and the relationships I had created my first three years built me up to this glorious moment. I picked up the skills of the people I surrounded myself with my first three years, and I improved upon my skills in the process. By the time I had started campaigning, my strategy was lined up to perfection, I got my team right, and we executed. The day before election results, The Student Government Association had their end of the year awards ceremony, and I won Bowie State Man of The Year. It meant the world being acknowledged by leaders of my campus but being crowned Mr. Bowie State University by the people was the greatest feeling ever. When you are moving in excellence, things will fall into place eventually, but you have to continue to strive. As I said, it's a constant journey. The next challenge must follow every accomplishment you have. Imagine excellence, believe excellence, strategize excellence, execute excellence, live excellence.

PART IX

FAMILY

"Family is like a bulletproof vest. They let you know that it is ok to be yourself in which reassures you of your safety. Be it blood or water; both play an essential part in your existence."

- Isaiah Daniels

Growing up, I came from a small family; I didn't have a lot of cousins that I hung around consistently. I have one sister and one first cousin. I'm beyond grateful for who was in my life growing up, and I wouldn't change a thing. When I got to Bowie State University, I didn't know anyone. It was like starting from scratch. However, it didn't take me long to find out I was going to be adding names to my family tree. Growing up, a wise man told me, "We don't have friends, we have family." What he meant was anyone you trust enough to call your friend, you should treat like family otherwise there was no reason for them to be around. I heard that phrase so many times through High School, but I felt it when I got to college. It started in my freshman seminar class, Dr. Shorter always liked the words of encouragement I had for the class. So the class decided to have me start praying for us at the conclusion of every class. It became our way of showing appreciation for each other and caring for each other before we would part ways. This felt like family because I was used to praying with my family at home, but they weren't around, so this time, my class filled that void immediately. I had gotten so close to my classmates they started to ask me if I needed a place to stay for the holidays because they knew I was from California. My second year, I wanted to stay around and get an internship; my brother, Marcus's family opened up their house to me for the whole summer. My final year, my pockets were hurting. My brother, Brian, and his wife opened their house up to me for the first semester, and Dr. Shorter let me stay with him for the second semester. I can't fully explain how great the feeling was having people that cared for me like this that I hadn't known long. All I can say is, I know that's what family is supposed to feel like. It was unconditional love from people who wanted to see me succeed.

I always wanted the house full of first cousins growing up, but I found that love in the friends who became family while I was at my HBCU. It made me realize having blood relation is great, and there is nothing like it. But, what determines who your family is, is love and loyalty. There are no blood restrictions on that. I thank God for the opportunity I was blessed with to step into my rites of passage on that campus; because I came out on the other side with an additional family tree. These people pushed me, argued with me, held me accountable to be the best version of myself the way family is supposed to. There's nothing I wouldn't do for them and vice versa.

Life is complicated for all of us, so I think the best thing you can do is put yourself in a position to build a support system around you that will genuinely love you. There is no love like HBCU love, everything you've heard about it being extremely family-oriented is accurate. There's a misconception that a family-oriented environment means the people around you don't challenge you. They challenge you more. The result of having a campus full of black teachers, administration and students is more people are going to see themselves in you. We see so much negativity about ourselves in media that sometimes, we fall into believing it. Believing we aren't smart enough or there is too much stacked against us. That doesn't work at an HBCU because most of the people around you have gone through the same things, they are dealing with that same stereotypes, and they're still finding a way to get the job done. Excuses don't survive on the HBCU campus because we know our greatness and we see it in everyone walking the campus. The family has big expectations, and they will not accept any less. You have to decide if you want the environment where you have a reminder of the greatness within you every day and living up to that or if you want to take another route where you'll be expected to graduate, but they may not push you towards fulfillment.

Whenever I do a seminar, one of the questions that always comes up is, "What about diversity?" The interesting part is you very rarely hear white people or any other group of people use this as a reason to get away from their people. The beauty of attending an HBCU is getting a full display of the "Black Family" on a global scale. You get to learn about black people from all over the world. What they eat, what music they listen to, how they dress, how their lifestyles or religions differ. It's one thing to have questions; it's another to be able to go straight to the source. When you can talk to a black Republican, a black Jew, a black homosexual or other blacks with interest you haven't come across. It exposes you to the similarities in all of us that should lead to breaking down the barriers that prohibit us from having a constructive dialogue. These are the conversations HBCU students have every day, and they help build a tight-knit family. The family doesn't stop on campus. It spreads throughout the HBCU circle. Being a part of the HBCU family is a fraternity/sorority in itself; we protect each other, we have fun with each other, we have rivalries with each other, but we don't allow outside parties to say anything bad about us. I'll give you two examples; I visited Lemoyne-Owen College and got the opportunity to meet some of the administration. I told them I was Mr. Bowie State University a few years ago. They asked to see a picture, and I showed them one. They walked me to the student store, opened it up on a day it was closed, and let me pick a few things out for free to take home. When I've worn my UCLA stuff around and met people who went to other predominantly white institutions, I've never received the same love I got from people who attended HBCUs. There's a different set of rules, beliefs, and comradery that can't be duplicated by predominantly white institutions. They're great schools, but the family spirit that comes along with the HBCU culture is a once in a lifetime opportunity. I go back to the east coast or down south and never have to pay for a hotel because of the family I've made in college. That love is second to none.

PART X

PURPOSE

"Purpose is what you owe this world. We're all born with debt, something that we must pay forward. We spend our lives trying to find exactly what it is that we owe. Those who don't know or have yet to figure that out struggle to find themselves. Struggle to find their purpose: the very thing that we owe to this world and ourselves."

- Devin Davidson

What is the essence of your existence? The essence of your existence is the lock securing your future. The key to that lock is a constant purpose. What do you want to do? Who do you want to be? What will be your mark on the world? When I was leaving High School, all I knew was I wanted to be a businessman. Russell Simmons was my role model in High School, I appreciated how he represented ownership as a black man, how he built products from the ground up and brought something unique to every field he entered. Reading his book, "Do You", my senior year only increased my admiration for him and his work. But, where do I start? How do I become that great businessman? Who do I want to lead? These should be questions you are thinking about or already answered. You also need to figure out the difference between your gift and your Purpose. Sometimes, they're the same thing, but sometimes, they aren't. Your gift is something that comes naturally to you, you're great at it, and it can get you paid. But, your purpose is what gives you life, gets you up every day and brings fulfillment to your life. That fulfillment is what makes life complete, makes you feel whole.

As I was going through college, I had no idea what my purpose was. I knew what I was good at; communicating and bringing people together. My HBCU helped me realize my purpose. I connected with some other great minds, and we created a group called Black Male Agenda. The significant part about HBCUs is you get surrounded by so many like minds. For a black man or black woman, there is no better place to find like minds than an HBCU.   Being around so many like minds raises confidence in you and makes you want to build your level to unseen heights. We settled on a collective purpose. I knew it was right. It felt right. More than that I believed in it, belief is the first part of the equation, it builds an irresistible desire to fulfill the purpose by any means necessary. The purpose I found was changing the world. Sounds crazy, right? I believe I can change the world. I think you can too. I don't have a doubt about it. You shouldn't have any doubts about where your life is headed either. If you do have doubts, you need to start surrounding yourself with people who can help you find what's missing from your life to bring purpose in it.

My HBCU has played a vital part in instilling the confidence and belief I have in myself to change the world. My teachers, my friends, and my mentors at my HBCU were the driving force I needed to go from good to great. My HBCU was the place I needed to get to so I could prepare myself mentally, spiritually and physically to take on the challenge of changing a world that needs healing. I believe we are all here to change the world. You have to find the way you want to connect with the world, strategize, then move forward with implementing the change you want to see in the world. Don't waste your time living a life you won't love, find your purpose and you'll find God's gift for you. Use It.

EPILOGUE

Thank you for taking the time to read what I believe will be a crucial component in the college selection process for black people from now on. I also think it will be an excellent resource for counselors and parents who want to get an idea of why HBCUs can be beneficial for all students. These great institutions have been providing us with opportunities to learn and have prepared more black people in America for professional positions than any other kind of universities. These great institutions are vital pieces of black culture that we must protect at all cost. Even if you decide not to attend one of them, understand the history that must be preserved and built upon. Our ancestors put blood, sweat, and tears into these great places. We must support.

To know where you're going, you have to see where you've been. We build upon the legacy of our ancestors with the hope that one day, someone coming behind us will build upon the legacy we've created. Handle your responsibilities by aligning yourself with the stars and by striving for what seems impossible to the ordinary. It may be for them but remember, you are extraordinary.

Top 7 Resources for the HBCU Experience:

1. The Black College Expo (Dr. Theresa Price)

2. 100% College Prep HBCU Tour (Diane Gray)

3. HBCU HUB APP (Jonathan Swindell)

4. School Days (A Spike Lee Joint)

5. Tell Them We Are Rising: The Story of Black Colleges and Universities (Documentary by Stanley Nelson)

6. Kanye West - School Spirit

7. Stomp The Yard (Movie by Will Packer and Rob Hardy)

Made in the USA
Monee, IL
28 January 2024

51897038R00038